Published by 331 Enterprises, LLC
www.331enterprises.com

ISBN: 979-8-9940524-4-0

Illustrations by Elga Ismaili
Printed in the United States of America.

My Heart Still Remembers Daddy is a work of love and remembrance based on family experiences of grief, healing, and the lasting bond between a child and her father.

DEDICATION

For Dustin Klug —
my beloved husband,
and Aaliyah's amazing daddy
who now watches over us from heaven.

Your love shaped our family,
and your memory lives in every page of this book.
As we walk forward without you,

you're still here —
in our laughter,
in our tears,
and in our hearts.

This story is for you…
and a reminder that the love you left
never left us.

— Delilah & Aaliyah

MY HEART STILL REMEMBERS DADDY

Sometimes I close my eyes,
and I remember the way Daddy's arms felt—
safe and warm,
like my favorite blanket after a long day.

Even though he's not here now,
my heart still remembers.
It remembers his laugh,
his stories,
and the way he called me "Princess."

Some days, I miss him so much.
At school, I get quiet sometimes—
not because I'm sad,
but because I'm remembering.

Sometimes I still cry.
Sometimes I still wish.

But I also laugh,
and sing,
and run really fast.
Daddy was one of my biggest fans.

And even though he's gone,
his love didn't leave.
It lives right here in me.

At night, everything slows down,
and that's when I miss him most.

Some nights Mom tells me stories about
Daddy—
how he played his guitar
and got lost in the melody,
and how he made my bacon
just the way I liked it.
Nobody can make bacon the way he could.

I miss that.
I miss him.
Sometimes I hold my favorite stuffed
bunny tight.
It helps me a little.

I close my eyes and whisper,
"I love you, Daddy."
I hope the stars carry it to him.

Mom and I made a memory box.
We filled it with little things—
his work badge, a penny from heaven,
a yellow rose, and a picture of us
on the swings he built me.

When I'm outside on those swings,
I imagine he hears me.
I tell him about my day,
my friends,
and how much I miss him.

Every single day,
my heart still remembers Daddy.

In the summer, our family always had a water balloon fight.
Daddy was the best at that game.
We laughed so much together.

Sometimes I wonder,
"Will I always feel like this?"
"Will the missing ever stop?"

Mom says love never goes away.
It just finds new ways to stay—
like a whisper in the wind
or a warm feeling I get
when I see a picture of us
and smile.

One day, I laughed so hard
I forgot to be sad—
just for a second.
Then I felt guilty,
like laughing meant forgetting.
But Mom said Daddy would
want me to laugh.

Sometimes we dance in the kitchen—
Mom, me, and the music.
And sometimes,
it feels like Daddy is dancing too.

I asked Mom if Daddy still loves me from heaven.
She smiled,
with tears in her eyes,
and said,
"Love like his never leaves.
It just finds new ways to stay."

So now I look for him in the little things—
the sun warming my face,
the wind whispering through the trees,
and the sparkle in the stars
when I say his name.

Even though Daddy isn't here
the way he used to be,
my heart still remembers.
It always will.
Every single day.

♡ Author's Notes from Aaliyah ♡

Writing this book with my mom has been really special.
We've been through a lot together, and working on this story
made us smile again.
It helped me remember my dad and all the ways that make my
heart feel full —
even when it also hurts.

This book is about love that doesn't disappear.
It's about missing someone so much,
but still finding ways to carry them with you.
I hope every kid who reads this knows it's okay to cry,
to laugh,
and to remember someone you love in your own way.

Because when someone you love becomes a memory…
that memory becomes part of your heart forever.

— Aaliyah Klug

A Note From Us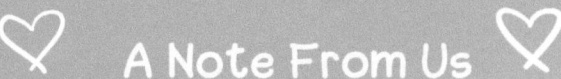

We wrote this book to help children and grown-ups remember
that love never really leaves us.
It lives on in the laughter,
the quiet moments,
the bedtime talks,
the memories we hold close,
and the stars we whisper to at night.

We hope this story gives children who lost someone they love
a place to feel seen,
a place to understand,
and a place to know that grief is not the end of the story.

There is still love.
There is still joy.
There is still hope.

And yes — there is still memory.
The kind that wraps around your heart like a soft hug
and stays with you always.

— Delilah & Aaliyah Klug

The End